Organize Your Day: Live Your Life By Design & Not Default - Learn How To Manage Your Day, Become More Productive, and De-clutter Your Life

Mai Jun
© 2015

Disclaimer

Table of Contents

Introduction

Do you feel that there should be more to life? Has your life become a blur of activity doing things that you have to do, with little time to do what you actually want to do? You are not alone – for most Americans, time is the one thing that seems to come in a very short supply.

If you want to get more out of life, starting right this instant, you need to learn how to more effectively manage your time. This book will help you do that.

The good news is that you can go from harassed to happy by simply practicing better time management and organizing your day more efficiently. Better time management can be as simple as having set times to check your emails or as complex as setting out a schedule for the whole week – it really depends on what it is that you need right now.

This book is going to teach you how to manage your time better, how to prioritize your tasks and how to be a lot more efficient when it comes to managing at home and at work. You will learn techniques that are very easy to apply and that can really assist when it comes to reducing your time deficit.

We will go through how to deal with time wasters and procrastination, getting your mindset right and what mistakes are commonly made when it comes to time management.

Time has become a very precious commodity and it seems to be something that we are becoming increasingly short of. There are just too many things that seem to be vying for our attention and most people just find that they run out of hours in the day.

Whether you want to give yourself an extra competitive edge or simply just spend less time running yourself ragged, effective time management can help you.

So, let's not waste any more time on the introduction and let's get right down to the information that you need.

Why Organize Your Day Anyway?

When I first moved out of my parent's house, I was very disorganized. (At the time, I said that I was just spontaneous and creative.) This was not too much of an issue when I was starting out as I had an entry level position.

As I started moving up the ranks though, this became more and more of a problem. My desk on any given day was typically a mess and, although I pretty much knew around about where everything was, a lot of time was wasted wading through piles of stuff looking for what I needed to work on.

My apartment was also a bit messy. Again, at first, this did not present much of a problem. As I started accumulating more and more stuff though, I started to realize that I needed to do something.

The turning point for me was not a major event at all – I needed to file some papers and could not find a punch. This was ridiculous because I knew that there were two punches in the apartment somewhere.

I ended up buying another one and that was the moment when I realized that things had gotten too out of control. Filing a few bills had taken me around about three hours – two and a half of which were spent looking for the punch and about twenty minutes of which were wasted in buying a new punch.

Tote in the money spent buying a new punch, and the cost of driving to the store and this new punch became a bit of a costly exercise, especially since it was such an unnecessary expense.

Being Organized Saves You Time

Being disorganized means that somewhere along the line you are wasting time. Whether that is because you are constantly looking for stuff or whether it is because you simply take on a lot more than you should, you will find that time is wasted.

Five minutes of time saved here and there may not sound like a lot, it may not even sound that important but all those little blocks of time saved add up – increasing the amount of time available to you.

Using your time more efficiently allows you build your competitive edge in the workplace and can mean saving your sanity at home as well.

Your time is important – use it wisely.

Being Organized Can Save You Money

There are two ways that being organized actually saves you money. For starters, time that is wasted is effectively time that could be put to much better use.

Let us say that you are spending a half an hour four times a day to check and read your emails. That is two hours spent on emails in one day. If you reduce that to a half an hour in the morning and mid-afternoon, you are effectively giving yourself an extra hour to work on more important issues like actually acting on those emails or doing something that could help to advance your career.

With fewer distractions, you are able to cope with your workload and are liable to feel less stressed out. The less stressed you are, the more productive you are and, consequently, the more time you will save.

Leisure time saved is just as important as work time saved – you benefit from more leisure time as it helps to reduce your overall stress levels.

The other way that you save money by being organized is actually in the dollars that you don't waste. My example of having to buy a new punch may seem insignificant but it could just as easily have been something more expensive.

Whenever you have to pay late fees, replace an item that you simply cannot find, etc. you are basically wasting money needlessly.

Being Organized Means Being Less Stressed

Efficient time use means that you will get more done in the amount of time that you have allotted to you. That means that you will be more productive and less stressed in both your work and home lives.

Think about it for a second – that fifteen minutes that you spend looking for your keys every morning could be spent taking a walk around the block or with your kids.

Some people mistake being organized with being too much of a perfectionist but, once you get the hang of it, it becomes a valuable tool in helping you to reduce the stress in your life.

Getting Your Mindset Right

For me, it meant changing my outlook and the way that I thought about things. My mother was a highly organized person and I think that part of the reason that I became disorganized was, in part, a form of rebellion against the very structured lives that we lived growing up.

I also found that this rebellious streak reared its head at work when my co-workers would offer to help me "sort out" my desk. One time, one of my co-workers tidied up for me when I was out for lunch and I was furious.

What I did realize is that I had to change my attitude – being organized was a choice that was going to make a positive change in my life. It was not easy at first but, once I got my mind around this concept, it became a lot easier and being organized became more of a habit than a burden.

I also found that I had to actively look for ways to streamline everything and this meant a shift from simply dealing with things as they came up to actually planning ahead to deal with them.

Don't Be A Yes Man

One area where I also had a problem was that I would take on things for other people, even when I neither had the time or interest in them, simply because I did not want to disappoint them.

Most of us have this desire to be helpful and feel that if we say "No", we won't be liked. The problem with this way of thinking is that, eventually, you are more likely to be taken for granted.

If you are constantly taking on extra assignments for your co-worker or looking after your neighbor's kids, eventually they will become so used to you doing this that it will be expected of you in future. The problem then is that if you, at that stage, say "No", it is much more likely to cause an issue.

You want to be able to help your friends and colleagues when you can but do ensure that you are not taking on too much. People who care about you will understand that you cannot do everything and those that do not are not worth wasting your time on anyway.

Where Does Your Time Go?

For the upcoming week, you are going to record everything that you do and how you are feeling at the time. Now, if you are already battling to get everything done as it is, it may seem like a complete waste of time to do this – after all, who has the time?

I am going to insist that you keep this diary though – the week will go by very fast and, at the end of the week, you will be able to actually see why it is that you have no time to do what you want or need to do.

You might even be surprised to find that you actually have a lot more time than you though that you had because this will lay out for you in black and white where time has been wasted and it will also help you to identify the triggers of time wastage.

Did you really work all day or did you spend half an hour chatting to one of your colleagues or messing around on Facebook?

For me, the time diary was a real eye-opener. It had never previously occurred to me that the reason that I kept on running out of time was that I was wasting a lot of time myself.

The diary will help you to determine whether or not procrastination is a problem for you, what internal and external time wasters are in play and areas that could use some improvement in terms of priorities.

You will also have a black and white record of everything that you do for other people and, if you are one of those people who really hate to say, "No", this could be an invaluable eye opener for you.

Have a look at those tasks that you gave priority to. Where they essential to your success? If you are spending 80% of your time dealing with things that are only essential to results around about 20% of time, you are spending too much time on these things.

Your time diary is a written record that will show you how your day is spent. It is amazing how much time we spend on things that do not really matter in the long run.

Use your time diary to identify areas of weakness and areas that could be improved upon. Initially, you will only keep this diary for a week but you can always, if you like, keep it going for even longer than that.

Step 1: Identify And Deal With Time Wasters - Procrastination

This is one of the most important steps when it comes to actually saving yourself time. No matter how busy you are, there is a really good chance that you do waste time throughout the day.

Sometimes it is really obvious – like spending too much time on Facebook – and sometimes the lines are blurred a bit – like when you check your work email constantly. (This might seem as though you are trying to be more effective by dealing with emails as they come in but it is actually a time waster.

Procrastination Is The Worst Time Waster

Most of us procrastinate to some degree or another. You probably even realize that you are doing it but it might not seem like a big deal. The problem is that by putting things off to another time, you are simply increasing your own stress and may even be robbing yourself of opportunities down the line.

Let us say, for example, that you have a report that must be written by Friday and that you decide to put it off until Thursday. Not only will you need to scramble in order to get the work done on time, and so feel a lot more stressed, but you will not be able to take advantage of other opportunities that come your way. (What if your partner wants to take you out to a nice dinner or your boss wants you to sit in on training?)

It is far better to get things done as soon as we can, rather than putting them off until the last minute.

Believe me, I know that this can be difficult. I personally do not enjoy housework but, when I have work to do, it is amazing how I notice that the books in the bookshelf need to be alphabetized or how the drapes need to be washed.

And the worst thing about these urges to procrastinate is that, at the time, they do seem fairly reasonable. Your mind can actually come up with some very logical reasons to procrastinate.

It is said that we procrastinate for one of a few reasons – we are either afraid that we will fail or we are afraid that we will succeed. The basic driver behind this procrastination is thus fear. It can also be that the task at hand is boring or too difficult.

Fortunately, you can train yourself to identify these stalling tactics. Most of the time, all you need to do is to force yourself to get started on the task in order to be able to complete it in a timely fashion.

Beating Procrastination

Taking a little time to try and understand the motivation behind the procrastination is a good way to help you overcome it. What is the payoff for not doing the task now? What is the payoff if you do? Are you concerned that you are not capable of doing the task?

In some cases, doing a simple benefit analysis will be enough to motivate you to get started but this is not always the case. If the benefits of completing the task at hand do not seem to outweigh the benefits of putting it off in your mind, then you might need to look a little deeper and see what fear is actually at work.

Once you start recognizing these behaviors and the motivation behind them, it becomes easier to overcome them.

Another problem that procrastinators tend to have is that they are not really in tune with the amount of time that it will take to get through the task at hand. They may feel that it will take fifteen or twenty minutes, rather than a few hours and this is often what gets them into more trouble.

Quick Tip to Beat Procrastination: As mentioned earlier, if you are able to force yourself to get started, there is a good chance that you will make good progress on the task. If you are battling with procrastination, get yourself a timer and set a time limit for working on the task. Say to yourself that you will work on the report for ten minutes, for example, and set the timer accordingly. If you like, at the end of the ten minutes, you can allow yourself to get up and do something else.

More often than not, once you overcome that initial sense of inertia, you will find that you are quite happy to continue with the task at hand. By setting a time limit initially, you make the task seem less onerous in your mind. Working on the report for ten minutes, for example, seems a lot more manageable than working on it for a few hours.

It is also important to actually sit and time tasks that you need to repeat often so that you know how long they may take in future. That way, you have more realistic expectations when it comes to finishing tasks off.

Step 2: Identify And Deal With Internal Time Wasters

The Internet/ Email/ Social Media

Social media is fun, isn't it? So is surfing the web and going through your emails. The problem is that, unless you set specific limits on the amount of time that you will spend with these sites, you will end up wasting quite a bit of time.

My own personal weakness are when it comes to Pinterest and Facebook – I know that if I just jump into either site, I can lose hours out of my day really easily.

Here is what I find most helpful in dealing with these time wasters:

Email: I work from home and it used to be a pet peeve with my family that I would constantly be checking my phone for emails. Whether you are at work, or at home, set specific times of the day to read your email and ignore it the rest of the time, unless you know that something urgent is coming through. This may seem like a small issue but if you are looking up from your desk every twenty minutes or so to check your emails, you are actually losing your focus and will have to start again on the project that you were working on. Do yourself a favor and switch off desktop notifications that let you know when you have mail. Silence the notifying beep on your phone for the same reason.

The Internet: The internet is a huge place with tons and tons of interesting information. You need to be disciplined when surfing the web, especially when it comes to work circumstances. Look for the information that you need for the task at hand and then sign out.

Social Media: This is one area that does manage to ensnare a lot of us and this is a great shame. Using your personal social media accounts at work is a complete no-

no but it is something that a lot of us do. For me, Pinterest is my absolute favorite site and one that I can spend hours on at a time. Now, I am not saying that we must cut out social media altogether – it can be a great way to keep in contact and source new ideas. If you want to minimize its impact in terms of time wasting, you will need to pull out the timer again and set it. I allow myself ½ an hour a day each for Pinterest and for Facebook. When that half an hour is up, I switch to doing something else.

Are You Being Too Perfect?

This is something that a lot of people with time management issues suffer from – the desire that everything should be completely perfect.

I had a friend that always battled to get her reports in on time. It wasn't because she had not done the work. In fact, she usually finished it off a day or two ahead of time. What happened though was that she would read it through several times and then decide to rewrite bits, or she would waste time looking for the absolute perfect font. A report that should have taken a few hours to write took her days.

I am not saying that we should not aim to get our work looking professional but if you are finding that you have trouble getting tasks completed on time and that you feel that the work is never really good enough, it might be time to acknowledge that this is a problem – will anything ever be perfect enough in your eyes?

Fortunately, this is something that you can, once again, work on. Finish your next report and proofread it once only. Then give it to a friend or colleague to have a quick look over it. You are probably going to be pleasantly surprised that they also believe that it was well done.

There is a difference between being a perfectionist and being effective. Ask yourself whether the value that being a perfectionist brings into your life outweighs the negatives of being less efficient.

Step 3: Identify And Deal With External Time Wasters

External Time Wasters

We have all been there – you have a ton of work on your plate and Suzy from accounting stops by for a chat. Before you know it, half an hour is gone and your work is piling up even more.

If you are lucky, you have an office door that can be shut and can put up a do not disturb sign. For those of us who do not have that luxury, however, things become a touch more difficult.

Co-Workers: If you have co-workers who are stopping by for a quick chat, it is better to be perfectly honest – "Hi, I would love to discuss that with you but I am really up against a tough deadline – how about we talk about it over lunch?" No one could take offence to that and the chatty people in your office will quickly cotton on to the fact that you are working and should not be disturbed.

If your trips to accounting always end up in getting you embroiled in a long conversation, then you need to nip the conversation in the bud in a tactful manner or make sure that you only go to accounting when it is absolutely necessary.

Clients: When it comes to clients that are taking up too much of your time, the situation can be a bit trickier. You do not want to come right out and say that you do not have time for them.

In these instances, there are non-verbal cues that you can use to hasten things along. Standing up, for example, is a strong cue that the interview is done and, if the person is at all sensitive to such things, they should also stand up.

You can also begin to walk towards the door, again this will signal to most people that the interview is over.

Should none of the non-verbal cues work, you will need a more direct approach, "Well, I have really enjoyed chatting to you but I am afraid that I have another appointment due soon. Can we take this up again next time?" As long as you are tactful, your client will not feel as though they are being shunted aside.

Family and Friends: This will mainly apply if you are working from home. The problem here is that many people think that because you are working from home, you have plenty of time to goof off. If only that were the case.

In this instance, it is important that you set some ground rules when it comes to family and friends. Explain to them that, whilst you would love for them to be able to drop by whenever they feel like it, that you are actually working and need time to concentrate on the business at hand.

Set actual business hours so that your family and friends know when they can drop up and when they should not.

Step 4: Identify What Is Urgent And Important

How much of your day is spent working on things that are neither urgent nor important? To really get ahead when it comes to time management, you need to start categorizing the tasks that you need to accomplish in terms of priority. First list tasks that are urgent, then tasks that are important. These tasks are the ones that you should spend time on during the day.

After that, look at the rest of your tasks – Are they important? (Like rewriting the report for the third time?) Are they urgent? Like re-alphabetizing the books on your bookshelf.

If a task is neither urgent nor important, and you are short of time, why would you consider doing it?

And, if there is a reason to do it anyway – like your boss told you to do it, how much time are you going to devote to it?

Importance Vs Urgency

Breaking tasks up in this manner will already make your life a lot easier so that you get what is urgent and important out of the way first.

What happens though if you have one task that is urgent and one task that is important? How then do you decide which one ought to be done first?

In this instance you will need to consider two things – how long each task will take and how urgent both tasks are.

If the important task, for example, will take a few minutes, it might just pay to get it out of the way so that you can concentrate on the urgent task.

On the other hand, if the urgent task is extremely urgent, you may to get that over and done with first.

When you seem to have too much to accomplish in a day, splitting your tasks into different categories:

Ask yourself:

Is this urgent and important?

Is this urgent but not important?

Is this important but not urgent?

Is this neither important nor urgent?

The lower down your task is on that scale, the less attention it should be getting from you.

Beware Of False Urgency

A big problem in society today is that it is the "in" thing to be stressed out. Just do a little experiment – tell someone you know well how stressed you are feeling and note their response. Chances are, although they will no doubt commiserate with you, they will also let you know how stressed they are.

For a lot of people, being stressed out has become a bit of a status symbol – something that basically indicates that the person is so successful that they have no time for anything else.

Be careful in your own life of falling into this trap – as nice as it can be to fit in, this is one area where fitting in is not going to do you any favors.

Look at your list of tasks – do you really need to do all of that or are you trying to create a never-ending list of projects so that you can look busier?

Step 5: Get Organized

Now that you know what your potential problems are, it is time to start getting a plan together to deal with them.

If, for example, Facebook is a big time waster during the day, find out whether you can block it between certain hours. We have already touched briefly on dealing with intrusions to your day so now you have an idea as to how this will work.

Being organized and more efficient is more about knowing what may come up and having a plan in place to deal with it when it does, than being super-efficient.

Let's face it, when you first get started on this, it will be easy to switch off the Facebook or ignore your instant messages. What about when the motivation starts to wane though? What if you are having a really bad day?

It is for times like these that a good plan of action is really important. As far as possible, get rid of as many of the external distractions as you can.

Also try to limit your exposure to things that will end up being a waste of time and find alternative was to deal with stressors that drive you to these things.

Communicate your plan with those that you live and work with so that they know what is going on. Perhaps you would prefer not to see all those funny emails or you no longer want to spend half an hour a day griping about the boss – be open and honest in a tactful manner to the people around you so that they can also help you out in this.

In the upcoming chapters, we will deal with more specific tricks and tips to help you out at home and work.

How To Organize Your Family

Now that you have some idea what the time wasters in your life are, it is a good idea to take to get those family members who are able to to also complete a time diary.

The most important thing when it comes to getting your family on board with getting more organized is to get their buy in. This means that you may need to explain the benefits for each member personally. If they complete the time diary, they can see for themselves where the main issues are.

You can then, as a family, hold a brainstorming session to see where time management as a whole can be improved.

Here are some other tips that you and your family can use to make things go a lot more smoothly at home:

A weekly schedule: A weekly schedule is a must, especially if all the family members have a number of different activities that they are involved in. By setting this schedule up on a Sunday night, you can more effectively plan your week – arranging for lifts for kids or combining lift club and shopping duties.

Combine resources: Can you get a lift club started with your neighbors? What about the other parents at the school? Combining resources with friends and families make it a lot easier to get more done – perhaps your parents could fetch and carry the kids from soccer practice once a week, for example, they get chance to spend time with their grandkids and some of your load is reduced.

Everyone must do their bit: It is a big stereotype that the wife is the one that does all the cooking and cleaning. Whilst this is certainly not always the case anymore, there is a good chance that one person is primarily responsible when it comes to cleaning or tidying the home. Everyone needs to give a hand here – whether that means picking up their toys or helping to straighten out the lounge.

Each person in the family needs to get used to putting their dishes either into the sink or dishwasher and everyone must put their own clothes into the laundry hamper.

Have a small basket in each room for items that need to be put in a different room – that way, putting things to right again will be a lot easier.

Make it a rule that everyone picks up one or two items to put away when moving from room to room.

Designate areas for certain tasks: By this I mean having a basket at the door for keys to be put in as soon as each person comes home. Once everyone gets used to keeping the keys at a central location, there will no longer be any reason to have to waste time in the morning hunting them down.

By the same token, have an in-basket for your kids to put permission slips, reports, etc. into so that you can see them in plenty of time to take action.

Watch out for clutter: Clutter can effectively drain your energy – the worse it gets, the worse it makes you feel. Get everyone into the habit of putting stuff away when they have finished using it and you will find that the house becomes a lot neater and tidier naturally.

Before you or anyone in the family buys something, you should have an idea of where it will be put. If possible, for every item that comes in, one should go out.

Organize Your Work Place

This is not quite as easy as organizing your home but similar principles do apply. To start off with, being open and honest with your colleagues about your new plan will go a long way to helping you out here.

Of course, there are going to be those who either forget or who simply aren't interested. If you have people constantly stopping by for a chat, you should firmly, but nicely, let them know that you have not got the time to do so.

After a while, even the most determined time wasters will get the message and move on to an easier target.

Designate set times: Start with setting a specific time to check your email – perhaps first thing in the morning and in the middle of the afternoon. If possible, set "office hours" for staff that need to refer things to you. Allot time throughout the day to tackle various regular tasks and, as far as possible, stick to these allotted times.

Another advantage of having completed the time diary is that you should now have an idea of when your optimal working times are – times that you feel most alert and ready to work. Schedule difficult tasks for these times during the day and leave the easier tasks for times when you are not at optimal capacity.

Writing that report, for example, may be better tackled when you have just gotten to work, rather than after you have had a long lunch break.

Tackling difficult tasks when your brain is more alert makes the process a lot simpler and means that it will go more quickly.

Your to do list: I am in two minds when it comes to having a to do list. On the plus side, you are reminded of what you have to do. On the negative side, you could end up with a list so long that you are put off even trying to complete everything on it.

Every morning, before you start your work day, take fifteen or thirty minutes to go through what it is that you need to do that day and plan your day in the most efficient way possible.

Find the top five most important and urgent tasks and put these on your actual to do list. Keeping the list short makes it seem less daunting and you have more chance of getting through it.

Any other items should be categorized in terms of importance and how urgent they are. Items that are neither important nor urgent should not make it onto your list.

Be realistic when it comes to drawing up this list because you do want to be able to feel that you accomplished something on a daily basis. Putting yourself under too much pressure with unrealistic goals will leave you open to failure.

Don't be afraid to tune out completely: If you have a really difficult task that you need to accomplish, switch off your phone and email and ask colleagues not to disturb you. It seems a little alien to us in this day and age that we can be out of contact but you would be amazed at how much you can get accomplished when you cut out the distractions.

Unhealthy Work Habits

In this chapter, we are going to go through some unhealthy work habits that could be sapping productivity right at this moment. If you find that you are doing some or all of these, don't feel too bad – these are pretty common behaviors.

Paper shuffling: When it comes to an unhealthy work habit, paper shuffling is the worst. Basically the paper gets picked up, read and put away again to be dealt with later. This is a huge waste of time – if possible, read what it is that you need to and deal with the email/ memo/ letter/ etc. immediately. For maximum efficiency, every paper should only be handled once before being filed.

Never challenging the established way of doing things: This is the "If it isn't broken, don't fix it mentality" and this can be very damaging to productivity. Look at the way things are being done in the office – the laid down procedures. Is there some way to streamline the process? As an example, a bank that I know of used to have carbonized deposit slips. The idea was that the bank would keep the original and the client would get a carbon copy as proof of deposit. When the bank went onto an automated system, it became standard practice for the tellers to print a copy of the deposit slip to attach behind the client's copy. What was crazy about this is that the client ended up getting two copies. But, that was the way things had always been done so it continued like that for a couple of years – until a teller actually raised the issue of the duplicate deposit receipt. She suggested providing a single slip of paper for the bank's records and that the client's receipt would be printed out when the deposit was made. Sounds like a small change, doesn't it? It saved the bank thousands every year.

The point that I am making here is that things change – what may have been considered best practice even two years ago, may no longer serve the company. I am not suggesting just throwing the policy book out of the window but I am suggesting that you look for better ways to do things.

Working harder and not smarter: We all know that if we put in the long hours and take on a lot of extra work, we will definitely be in line for some great promotions. The only problem when it comes to this is that, by the time we do get the promotions, we are so stressed out that we cannot enjoy it. You do have to do your work to get ahead but you can also look for shortcuts that work for you.

If you feel that you are drowning in work, or that you simply cannot cope, you need to ask for assistance. When I began to move up at work, I found that it became increasingly difficult to keep up with the workload. Despite this fact, if the boss asked me to add on some more work, I always said "Yes" and never said anything about being snowed under.

Eventually, I was getting in earlier every day, working through my lunch break and leaving late at night – taking work home most of the time. I even started to come in on my days off. It didn't help – in fact, it only seemed to make things worse. I became more and more tired and started to get ill. My capacity to put in long hours dwindled and eventually I found that I hated work. Even tasks that before had seemed easy now became really difficult to finish off.

There will be times that you will need to put in extra hours, that is a given, but you do also need to ensure that you get enough downtime as well. It is important to give yourself a bit of break during the day so, even if you cannot take a full lunch hour, do get up from behind your desk and take the time to have something to eat and a bit of a break.

If you have to take work home and come in on the days that you are off in order to catch up on your work, you have got too much work on your plate and something will need to be done to prevent your overall efficiency from suffering.

Take time to look after yourself if you want to be able to perform at your peak – this means eating properly, getting enough exercise and getting enough sleep. If you are constantly worrying about how much work needs to be done, you are not relaxing properly during your leisure time and it is a pretty safe bet that you are also not sleeping as well as you should.

You need to have some pretty strict rules in place to separate work out from your home life. These rules can be broken once in a while but this should be the exception rather than the rule.

Never saying no: As mentioned above, this is one of those habits that are very tough to break – we don't like disappointing others, after all. Saying yes when you actually do not have the time or inclination to help will only increase your stress levels and workload. You may even find that you do not do as good a job as you should as a result. Is it really worth so much to say "Yes" to everyone? Before saying "Yes", ask yourself two questions, "Do I want to do this?" and "Do I have the time to do this?" If need be, take a little time to think about it – tell the other person that you are not sure whether or not you will be able to help them out and see if you can take a little time to decide. If you decide against helping them out, a tactful and firm "No" needs to be communicated to them as soon as you possibly can. This allows them to make other arrangements.

Putting off unpleasant task as long as possible: Okay, so sifting through the sales stats for the last year is not the most fun job on the planet but it is something that you will need to do anyway. You could put it off but there will always be this feeling of unease in the corner of your mind knowing that it still needs to be done.

Schedule unpleasant tasks first thing in the morning and get them over and done with as quickly as possible. That way, you can enjoy the rest of your day.

Spending too much time online: This applies both at work and at home. All of us are guilty of this at some stage or another. Maybe Mabel from human resources has sent you a funny video to watch or maybe you have subscribed to some blog that sends weekly updates. If you are not careful, you might find that you have to deal with thousands of unnecessary emails a week. Take the time to go through your incoming mail and unsubscribe to any in the list that no longer interest you. If some of your contacts only ever send jokes or junk emails, add a filter so that these mails are put into a specified folder straightaway. If you feel that you do want to deal with these, they will be there for you to vet later.

As for those chain emails that go around, the easiest way to ensure that do not receive them is to not pass them on, ever. You don't want to be spammed, why do it to others?

Unhealthy Home Habits

When it comes to our home habits, we also tend to make a lot of mistakes that reduce our efficiency at home. In this chapter, we will deal with some of these.

Trying to be Super Mom or Super Dad: We all want to be the best parents we can possibly be but if that means that you are rushing around with hardly any time for yourself, you need to take a step back for a second. Your kids do need you – they also need you to be relaxed and calm. You need to look after yourself in order to be a better parent. That may mean delegating some of the responsibilities to your spouse or asking for help. There is nothing wrong with that.

Picking up after everyone: You work an eight hour day and then still come home to tidy the house, do the cooking, laundry, etc. while your kids and spouse just sit by and watch. It's time to speak up. If both you and your partner are working full time jobs, it is only fair that you split up the housework. When your kids are old enough to do chores, assign these to them – it helps to teach them the value of working and also will help to prepare them for living on their own.

Kids should always, from an early age, be taught to pick up their toys and pack them away when not in use and to put their clothes in the laundry basket. My spouse was particularly bad when it came to putting dirty clothes in the laundry basket and I decided that enough was enough so I stopped picking the clothes off the floor. When the underwear ran out, I was given a long lecture but I never had to pick up laundry off the floor again – after that, it was always put into the basket.

Organization is good for your family and it is a good skill for adults and kids alike to learn. By doing everything for your kids, you are actually not allowing them any growth in future.

Being dragged down by unimportant details: I once worked with a woman who got up at four o'clock in the morning in order to start cleaning the house. She was adamant that she had to vacuum the carpets and dust all the nick knacks on a daily basis. She would then make breakfast for the family and then go and work a full day. At night, she would make supper for herself and her husband in addition to cooking for her children – basically, the children would choose what they wanted to eat and she made that for them. After dinner, she would was the dishes and laundry and iron the clothes from the previous day. She got to bed after ten every night. When she told me that she was tired all the time, I could not say that I was surprised. I think that it is great that she loves her family so much but are you truly saying that it is necessary to vacuum and dust every single day? In our house, we dust and vacuum once a week most of the time.

For me, as long as the house is clean, I cannot be bothered wasting time on unimportant tasks such as vacuuming daily or ironing the sheets.

Now, I am sure that for most of you this is an extreme example but I am also sure that there are things that you are doing now that are more of a waste of time than beneficial. We want our homes to be a safe haven for our families and comfortable – not sanitized zones.

Are you being dragged down by unimportant details? The work smarter, not harder rule applies to the home as much as it does to work.

What would you rather be doing? Cleaning the house and obsessing over small details or spending more time with your family?

Conclusion

Being better organized is a wonderfully easy way to amp up productivity and to help you make the most of your leisure time as well. Effective time management is a skill that anyone can learn and one that anyone can master and the payouts far outweigh the initial effort.

Do you know someone who always seems to get everything done on time and never seems to be stressed out? How can they manage when you both have the same number of hours in the day? Their secret is simply effective time management and organization.

It is now time for you to put what you have learned in this book into practice and start leading a more productive life yourself.

I wish you the best of luck when it comes to the new, more organized you!

Finally, I would like to thank you for downloading this book and would ask for just one more moment of your time – I would love to know what you thought of this book so please review it on Amazon for me. I would really appreciate you taking the time to do so.

www.ingramcontent.com/pod-product-compliance
Lightning Source LLC
Chambersburg PA
CBHW070958180526
45168CB00003B/1197